Mike McKinley has produced a
accessible resource. Perfect for sc
Christian life and trying to take the
with wisdom, faithfulness and bibli

Josh Moody,
Senior Pastor, College Church in Wheaton, Illinois,
Founder and President of God Centered Life Ministries,
Author of several books including *Burning Hearts, Journey to Joy, No
Other Gospel*, and *Boasting*

BELIEVE

WHAT SHOULD I KNOW?

MIKE MCKINLEY
SERIES EDITED BY MEZ MCCONNELL

CHRISTIAN
FOCUS

Copyright © Mike McKinley 2019

paperback ISBN 978-1-5271-0305-4
epub ISBN 978-1-5271-0365-8
mobi ISBN 978-1-5271-0366-5

10 9 8 7 6 5 4 3 2 1

Published in 2019
by
Christian Focus Publications Ltd,
Geanies House, Fearn, Ross-shire,
IV20 1TW, Great Britain.

www.christianfocus.com

Cover and interior design by Rubner Durais

Printed and bound
by Bell & Bain, Glasgow

CONTENTS

PREFACE

I didn't really get much exposure to church until I was about 10 years old. My parents had started our family when they were teenagers, and they had to kill themselves to get us into a solidly working-class life. But we lived in a place where most of the people were very wealthy. So when I first started going to church, most of the people there were rich. Everyone at church seemed successful, put-together, and important (I know now that it was only an appearance, that rich people have problems too – but I didn't know that then). But it wasn't clear to me as a child whether it was possible for people who weren't rich to follow Jesus. What did the church have to say to people who were struggling to make it from day to day?

I became a Christian as a young man, and now serve as a pastor. The neighbourhood where I live is full of needy people – many are in the country illegally and are barely able to keep their heads above water. These people have a lot of needs, but even more than food and health care and education, they need to know God – who he is and what he has said about them and their lives. It's my prayer that this little book would help them (and you) to know God better.

MIKE MCKINLEY
Pastor, Sterling Park Baptist Church

SERIES INTRODUCTION

The First Steps series will help equip those from an unchurched background take the first steps in following Jesus. We call this the 'pathway to service' as we believe that every Christian should be equipped to be of service to Christ and His church no matter your background or life experience.

If you are a church leader doing ministry in hard places, use these books as a tool to help grow those who are unfamiliar with the teachings of Jesus into new disciples. These books will equip them to grow in character, knowledge and action.

Or if you yourself are new to the Christian faith, still struggling to make sense of what a Christian is, or what the Bible actually says, then this is an easy to understand guide as you take your first steps as a follower of Jesus.

There are many ways to use these books.

+ They could be used by an individual who simply reads through the content and works through the questions on their own.

+ They could be used in a one-to-one setting, where two people read through the material before they meet and then discuss the questions together.

+ They could be used in a group setting where a leader presents the material as a talk, stopping for group discussion throughout.

Your setting will determine how you best use this resource.

A USER'S KEY:

As you work through the studies you will come across the following symbols…

SAMUEL – At points in each chapter you'll meet Samuel and hear something about his story and what's been going on in his life. We want you to take what we've been learning from the Bible and work out what difference it would make in Samuel's life. So whenever you see this symbol you'll hear some more about his story.

ILLUSTRATION – Through real-life examples and scenarios, these sections help us to understand the point that's being made.

STOP – When we hit an important or hard point we'll ask you to stop and spend some time thinking or chatting through what we've just learnt. This might be answering some questions, or it might be hearing more of Samuel's story.

KEY VERSE – The Bible is God's Word to us, and therefore it is the final word to us on everything we are to believe and how we are to behave. Therefore we want to read the Bible first, and we want to read it carefully. So whenever you see this symbol you are to read or listen to the Bible passage three times. If the person you're reading the Bible with feels comfortable, get them to read it at least once.

MEMORY VERSE – At the end of each chapter we'll suggest a Bible verse for memorisation. We have found Bible memorisation to be really effective in our context. The verse (or verses) will be directly related to what we've covered in the chapter.

SUMMARY – Also, at the end of each chapter we've included a short summary of the content of that chapter. If you're working your way through the book with another person, this might be useful to revisit when picking up from a previous week.

MEET SAMUEL

Samuel was born in a world of violence. On the streets of his San Salvador neighbourhood only the toughest survived to see adulthood. He never knew his father, and almost every other boy he knew had joined a gang in order to find both protection and a sense of belonging. By the time he was a teenager, he was selling drugs and shaking down local merchants. In the course of business, he'd killed several people and even been shot once himself.

And yet, despite everything, gang life never felt like a good fit to Samuel. He hated the way he felt after taking drugs. The faces of the people he'd killed haunted him when he slept. He knew that he was going to be damned by God for the things that he had done, but he didn't know what else to do.

When his aunt sent him to the United States to live with an uncle, Samuel wanted a fresh start. Not long after he arrived, one of his teachers invited him to come to her church's youth Bible study. Reluctantly, he agreed, and it was there he heard the good news that Jesus had died to take away the guilt and punishment of anyone who trusted in Him. It was hard for him to imagine that God could forgive him for the terrible things he'd done, but after about a year he became a follower of Jesus.

WHAT'S THE POINT?

GOD is holy and more loving than we can imagine.

1. WHO IS GOD?

SAMUEL

Now Samuel is out of school and trying to work a 'straight' job. He's trying to grow as a Christian. At the same time, his old gang from back home has a growing presence among the Salvadorans in his new hometown. Some have reached out to him to make it clear they're not happy he left. Normally, the only way out of the gang is in a pine box; nobody just quits. His old friends mock him and his attempt to earn money doing honest work. Some gang leaders have been making veiled threats, and Samuel is beginning to wonder if any of this is worth it. He's even thought about taking his own life just to make everything stop.

STOP

What do you think could make Samuel's situation better? Why might it be tempting to go back to his old way of life?

ILLUSTRATION

When I was a teenager, there was a time when a local bully was making my life difficult. The kid was big and mean, and I didn't know what to do about it. But then my older brother came home on his holiday leave from the military. He was trained to be part of a Special Forces unit, and you could tell just by looking at him that he was not someone to mess with. When that bully got a look at my brother, he didn't bother me again. I didn't have to worry, because the toughest guy I knew was on my side.

In the same way, what Samuel needs to know is that even though these gang members *seem* tough and powerful, **God is the one who is ultimately in control of everything.**

THE ONLY GOD

 'For thus says the LORD, who created the heavens (he is God!), who formed the earth and made it (he established it; he did not create it empty, he formed it to be inhabited!): "I am the LORD, and there is no other"' (Isa. 45:18).

'Our God is in the heavens; he does all that he pleases' (Ps. 115:3).

We see some very important things about God in these two verses:

+ He is a God who **speaks** ('thus says the Lord'). In other words, God can be known. We don't have to guess what He's like or what He wants from us. It doesn't really matter what we *feel* or what we *want* God to be like; what matters is *what He says about Himself.*

+ He is the **creator.** We'll see more about this in a later chapter, but for now we need to see that God is the one who made the heavens, the earth and everything that lives in them. As the creator, He has the authority to tell everyone and everything how to act.

+ He is the **only God.** God is not the *best* among a group of rivals; He is God and there is no other. We do not have to figure out which God to go to for help; there's only one true option.

+ He is **in control**. He does whatever He wants to do and no one can stop Him. Everyone has had the experience of being opposed or frustrated, but God is not like that. He has the power to accomplish every one of His desires.

ILLUSTRATION

When our family is invited over to someone's home for dinner, we always have to remind our children that while they're in our friends' home, they must abide by their rules: take your shoes off at the door, no throwing a ball in the house, don't light anything on fire. Well, this whole world is God's 'house'; it all belongs to Him! As a result, we're all obligated to live according to His rules.

STOP

For Samuel, the problems in his life seem massive. How might he feel differently if he began to understand that God is in control of everything and everyone?

GOD IS THE HOLY JUDGE

'For I am the LORD your God. Consecrate yourselves therefore, and be holy, for I am holy' (Lev. 11:44).

When the Lord speaks to His people, He reminds them that He is their God. He also tells them to consider themselves as set apart and different from the surrounding nations (that's the idea behind that word 'consecrate'). Other people do whatever seems right to them, but God's people are supposed to be holy. Why? Because God Himself is holy.

When we say that God is 'holy,' we mean He is morally pure. You and I may be inclined to do things that are wrong, but God is not. He hates evil, sin, and immorality. He is pure and always does the right thing in every situation. As a result, God's people are supposed to be like Him. Just like children resemble their parents, so we are supposed to resemble our Father in heaven. He is holy, so His children (that's us!) should be holy, too; there's a family resemblance. Sin is supposed to be normal to the world around us but foreign to God's people. For somebody in Samuel's position, this means he cannot go back to his old way of life.

This even explains why his old friends from the gang have been giving him such a hard time. In the book of 1 Peter we read:

'For the time that is past suffices for doing what the Gentiles want to do, living in sensuality, passions, drunkenness, orgies, drinking parties, and lawless idolatry. With respect to this they are surprised when you do not join them in the same flood of debauchery, and they malign you; but they will give account to him who is ready to judge the living and the dead' (1 Pet. 4:3–5).

You can see the situation Peter was addressing—new believers were struggling with their old buddies and their old way of life. Back in the day, before they became followers of Jesus, life was all drinking parties and orgies. But Peter says the time for that is past. Since they're now God's people, they're supposed to be holy; they no longer join in and live that way.

And as a result, their friends were giving them a hard time. Isn't it amazing how little has changed in 2,000 years since Peter wrote this? There's a feeling of safety in a crowd. When everyone is getting drunk and sleeping around, it makes such behaviour seem acceptable, even normal. As long as no one says anything, people do what they want without feeling guilty or having their conscience flare up. But now these new Christians were refusing to do the things that they used to do, and as a result their old 'friends' were talking smack about them (Peter uses the word 'maligning').

Notice what Peter tells these believers. The one thing they need to understand is that everyone in the world will ultimately give an account to this holy God for how they've lived. He is the one who judges the living and the dead. That has a way of putting everything in perspective, doesn't it?

SAMUEL

It might seem like becoming a Christian has created a bunch of problems for Samuel, but in reality it's his old friends who have the biggest problem of all. They're going to face a holy, all-powerful God as their judge!

STOP

How should knowing that God is a holy judge help Samuel resist the temptation to go back to his old way of life? How should it help him tell his old friends why he no longer lives like they do?

GOD IS LOVE

'But you, O Lord, are a God merciful and gracious, slow to anger and abounding in steadfast love and faithfulness' (Ps. 86:15).

Is God a powerful and holy judge, or is He a loving Father? The answer, according to the Bible, is both. The good news for us is that the God who created us and who judges us is also kind and loving toward His people. If God used His power like a bully, it would be hard to see how the Bible could claim to be good news. But the truth is, God always exercises His power with love and kindness towards His people.

In Psalm 86 the psalmist tells us wonderful things about God's character:

+ He is **merciful**. He shows kindness to those in need.

+ He is **gracious**. He forgives and blesses those unworthy of His care.

+ He is **slow to anger**. God is holy, but He is also patient. He is angry at sin and injustice, but it's not an out-of-control, hair-trigger anger. In fact, God restrains His anger in order to allow people time to repent and seek His grace.

+ He **abounds in steadfast love**. God overflows with an unshakeable love for His people. God's love is so great that in one of the Apostle John's letters, he says that 'God is love' (1 John 4:16).

+ He **abounds in faithfulness**. God never fails to deliver on His promises. His love for His people is unshakeable and unbreakable. Other people might betray us or fade out of our lives, but the Lord is always faithful.

It may seem strange to our modern minds, but the authors of the Bible do not really seem to struggle with the idea that God is powerful, holy, and just. His righteous anger against mankind's sinfulness makes sense. What astounds them, however, is God's love. Why would someone so great, so infinite, and so holy stoop to love insignificant and messed-up people like us (see Ps. 8:3–4, Rom. 3:23–26)? Time and time again, God affirms His love for His people is not rooted in anything wonderful about them, but in His own loving character (Deut. 7:7–8, Jer. 31:3, Hosea 11:1). God loves the unlovely because He is love.

We'll see more in coming chapters about God's love for His people, especially as it is shown to us in the gift of His Son, but for now just notice that the God of the Bible is even better than any version of Him that we could imagine or create in our minds. He is a beautiful combination of every good thing: holy and forgiving, powerful and tender, majestic and loving.

STOP

When you think about God, what aspects of His character are harder for you to accept and believe? Which are easier?

MEMORY VERSE

'Have you not known? Have you not heard? The LORD is the everlasting God, the Creator of the ends of the earth. He does not faint or grow weary; his understanding is unsearchable. He gives power to the faint, and to him who has no might he increases strength.' (Isa. 40:28–29)

SUMMARY

What Samuel needs more than anything else is to understand who God is. His problems seem very big, and so he needs to know there is One who is bigger. The Lord is the only God, eternal and limitless. He does whatever He pleases. Since He is the One who created everything, He is our holy judge and the only One who has the right to determine how we should live. And here's the good news: this holy God is more loving than we can imagine. So we can be sure He will always show kindness to His people in their time of need.

WHAT'S THE POINT?

Jesus, GOD's son, is both GOD and man.

2. WHO IS GOD THE SON?

In the previous chapter, we began to talk about God. We said all kinds of important and true things about Him. But all of the things that we said about God so far are things a Muslim or a Mormon or a Jewish person would likely be able to affirm. We've not yet talked about perhaps the most important thing there is to say about God: He is triune (that is to say, He is 'three in one'). The Bible teaches that the one God who created everything exists in three persons: the Father, the Son, and the Holy Spirit.

Now, I'm going to be honest with you. When we talk about the Trinity (a name we give to God because He is three and one), we're swimming in the deep end of the pool. There are certain things about God that are difficult for us to understand, but that doesn't mean they're untrue or unimportant. And so our goal when we talk about the Trinity is to grasp those things we are able to grasp, and simply trust God for the rest.

Here's the Bible's teaching about the Trinity, summed up in three ideas:

+ **God is three distinct persons.** The Father, Son, and Holy Spirit are not forces or powers or energies; they are persons. Furthermore, they're *distinct* persons: the Father is not the Son, the Son is not the Spirit, the Spirit is not the Father, etc. Got it?

- **Each one of the three persons is fully God.** The Father, Son, and Spirit are each fully God. No one of the three persons is greater or lesser than the others. That's important; each one is as much God as the others.

- **There is only one God.** Christians don't worship three separate and distinct gods; we worship only one God. The three persons of the Trinity all have the same nature or essence; there are no rivalries or jealousy between them. The three persons are one. As somebody once put it, God is three 'who' and one 'what.'

 SAMUEL

Samuel lives in a multi-cultural area. In school, he had classmates from all sorts of other different religions. There was a lot of talk about how we all worship the same God just in different ways. How should the doctrine of the Trinity help Samuel think through this common idea? If his Muslim and Jewish neighbours don't recognize that the one God exists in three persons, are they *really* worshipping the same God?

 ILLUSTRATION

Maybe you've heard people try to illustrate the Trinity using an

egg (shell, yolk, white),

or water (ice, liquid, steam),

or a shamrock (three petals, one plant),

but each illustration fails to represent the entire truth. In fact, there are no illustrations that adequately represent the Trinity because there is nothing quite like Him in all the universe. But just because something is hard to understand doesn't mean it's impossible or untrue.

 'And when Jesus was baptized, immediately he went up from the water, and behold, the heavens were opened to him, and he saw the Spirit of God descending like a dove and coming to rest on him; and behold, a voice from heaven said, "This is my beloved Son, with whom I am well pleased"' (Matt. 3:16–17).

At Jesus' baptism, we see all three persons of the Trinity: God the Father speaks about His delight in the Son on whom the Spirit has come to rest. Later, we'll see how each person in the Trinity has a critical role to play in our salvation: the Father sends the Son to die for us (John 3:16), the Son gives up His life for us as a sacrifice on the cross (Gal. 2:20), and the Spirit applies that salvation to all of God's people (John 3:3–7).

In the first chapter we considered the nature and character of God the Father (even though you may not have realized it!). There we saw that He is the creator of all things, both an all-powerful judge and an all-loving Father. With the rest of this chapter, we're going to look at a few things that we need to know about God the Son.

JESUS IS FULLY HUMAN

If you read the accounts of Jesus' birth, it's clear to everyone around that this was no ordinary pregnancy and no ordinary child. Jesus was conceived in the womb of His mother Mary, a virgin at the time, by the power of the Holy Spirit (Luke 1:26–38). We're not told exactly how this happened; only that it did. Because Jesus was conceived in this unusual way, He could be born as a human, yet without sin (Heb. 4:15, 1 John 3:5).

Though Jesus didn't have a typical conception, the Bible is clear that He was completely and truly a human being with a real human nature.

He grew in His mother's womb and was born as an infant.

> *He grew in size and maturity like other children; He wasn't some kind of wizard child with spooky magical powers.*
>
> > *He became weary and tired like any other man; He couldn't kick a football any farther than you or me.*
>
> *He was thirsty and hungry; He had friends and went to dinner parties.*

He felt sadness and anger and happiness.

There's nothing to indicate that if you'd seen Him walking down the street you would have noticed anything unusual about Him.

 'By this you know the Spirit of God: every spirit that confesses that Jesus Christ has come in the flesh is from God, and every spirit that does not confess Jesus is not from God' (1 John 4:2–3).

In the early days of the Christian church, some people began to teach that the Son of God hadn't *really* become a man. Instead, they taught that He only *seemed* to be a human, but in reality He was some kind of spirit being. They taught this because they thought all physical things were inferior to spiritual things. They reasoned that God could never become a real human being.

But the Apostle John wants us to be very clear: that kind of teaching doesn't come from God. The truth is that Jesus has come in the flesh; He was a real, true, full human being.

JESUS IS FULLY GOD

 SAMUEL

A lot of people in Samuel's life believe something about Jesus. His uncle goes to church on the weekends and keeps a picture of Jesus in his car for good luck. Some of the guys in the gang wear a crucifix for protection. Some of the old ladies in the neighbourhood pray to Jesus for healing and blessings. So he often wondered: 'Is Jesus more than just a man who was a healer, a teacher, and a dispenser of blessings?'

According to the Bible, Jesus was far greater than that. He's God the Son who became a man. He's a complete and genuine human being—and yet He is also fully God. The authors of the Bible demonstrate this clearly by showing Jesus' characteristics and attributes that the Bible had previously shown to belong to God alone:

- *He is all-powerful.* When He calmed a raging storm, Jesus' disciples wondered, '*Who then is this, that he commands even winds and water, and they obey him?*' (Luke 8:25). The unspoken answer hangs out there: He is God himself! Only God can control the forces of nature (Ps. 135:6-7).

- *He is eternal.* Jesus once told His opponents that, '*Before Abraham was, I am*' (John 8:58). That sounds kind of strange, but his hearers knew what He meant. Abraham had died more than 2,000 years earlier, but Jesus was saying that He had been around before Abraham's day.

- *He is all-knowing.* Jesus knew people's thoughts (Mark 2:8) and the state of their hearts (John 6:64). The people who spent the most time with Jesus put it this way: '*Now we know that you know all things…*' (John 16:30). This can only be said about God Himself (Ps. 139:1-4).

- *He has all authority.* In the Old Testament, God's prophets would speak God's words, saying, 'Thus says the Lord.' But Jesus didn't speak like that; instead, He would say things like, 'Truly, truly, I say to you' (Matt. 5:26). He didn't appeal to a higher authority because no higher authority exists. Jesus spoke as God Himself.

- *He is worthy of worship.* If you read the Bible, you'll see nothing that gets condemned more than people who worship something other than God. But the Bible is clear: worshipping Jesus is a good idea (Matt. 28:9, Heb. 1:6, Rev. 19:10)! The only conclusion that makes any sense is that this is okay because Jesus is Himself the true God!

The New Testament doesn't hesitate to speak of Jesus as God. A few examples:

- *'To them belong the patriarchs, and from their race, according to the flesh, is the Christ, who is God over all, blessed forever. Amen'* (Rom. 9:5).

- *'...waiting for our blessed hope, the appearing of the glory of our great God and Savior Jesus Christ'* (Titus 2:13).

- *'But of the Son he says, "Your throne, O God, is forever and ever, the sceptre of uprightness is the sceptre of your kingdom"'* (Heb. 1:8).

WHY BOTH?

The teaching of the Bible is that Jesus is fully God and fully human. He is not half-man and half-God. He's not the Spirit of God controlling the body of a man. Instead, He's 100% God and 100% man. Those two natures are distinct; they don't meld into some kind of superhuman alien being. But those two natures are also united; Jesus is not a split personality where His divine nature does one thing and His human nature does another.

This is important for us to believe because if it were not so, Jesus wouldn't be able to save sinners. *Jesus has to be fully human in order to save human beings.* As we'll see in a future chapter, Jesus saves us both by obeying God in our place and also by taking the punishment that we deserve for our sins on Himself. Jesus took our punishment and gives us His obedience as a gift. He can only accomplish this if He is one of us. He has to be fully human in order to take humanity's punishment and give humanity His righteousness.

Jesus has to be fully God in order to reconcile us to God. If Jesus weren't God, He couldn't take on Himself our punishment. Only an infinite person could bear infinite guilt and sin and yet live. We need Jesus, the Son of God in human flesh, to stand like a bridge between the eternal God and sinful humanity. Jesus is that bridge; the biblical word is 'mediator.' If Jesus isn't God, then He cannot bring us to God. A Jesus who is less than fully divine would be unable to save us. No wonder the Bible keeps reminding us that we cannot save ourselves; salvation comes from God alone!

SAMUEL

Because Jesus is fully God and fully man, He is precisely the saviour that Samuel needs. Samuel was well aware that he had done terrible things; he knew that no ordinary man could solve his sin problem. But he also longed to be known by someone who could understand what his life had been like. As someone who is truly a man, Jesus can sympathize with Samuel's troubles and represent him before God the Father. As someone who is truly God, Jesus is able to take away all his sin.

MEMORY VERSE

'For there is one God, and there is one mediator between God and men, the man Christ Jesus, who gave himself as a ransom for all, which is the testimony given at the proper time' (1 Tim. 2:5–6).

SUMMARY

People have all kinds of foolish ideas about Jesus. But the Bible's teaching is clear (even if it can be hard to understand at times):

+ Jesus has two natures, a divine and a human nature.

+ Each one of those natures is complete. He is 100% God and 100% man.

+ Those two natures are distinct. He's not some kind of hybrid being who's a mixture of God and man. Instead, He's fully God and fully man.

+ Though He has two natures, Jesus is only one person. All of the things that are true of His human nature are true of Jesus and all of the things that are true of His divine nature are true of Jesus.

WHAT'S THE POINT?

The Holy Spirit works powerfully to build the Church.

3. WHO IS GOD THE HOLY SPIRIT?

 SAMUEL

There are church vans running all over Samuel's neighbourhood, picking people up for services and dropping them off afterwards. They all seem to have names that reference the Holy Spirit or Pentecost or both; many of them are in Spanish. When Samuel visited his uncle's church, people were dancing and yelling and falling on the floor, saying something about how the Spirit had come upon them. Samuel has never experienced anything like that, and he doesn't really want to. Who is the Holy Spirit and, why is He important?

WHO IS THE SPIRIT?

We can put it this way: the Holy Spirit is the third person of the Trinity. There are two important truths in that statement:

+ First, **the Spirit is a person.** When we hear the word 'spirit,' we sometimes think of a ghost or an invisible force. But the Spirit is a *person*; He is a 'He,' not an 'it.' The Bible shows the Spirit doing all sorts of things that we would think of as personal: knowing (1 Cor. 2:11), teaching (John 14:26), being grieved (Eph. 4:30), comforting (Acts 9:31), and praying on behalf of others (Rom. 8:26–27).

• *Second, the Spirit is God.* This is implied strongly in the way the authors of the New Testament speak of the 'Father, Son, and Holy Spirit' together (see Matt. 28:19 for just one example). Since the Father and Son are both God, it would be very strange if the Spirit were not God but still got included in that phrase! In Acts 5:3, Peter accuses a man of lying to the Holy Spirit. Then, in the next verse he tells the man that he has lied to God (Acts 5:4). To lie to the Spirit is to lie to God Himself!

Human relationships are often marked by tension and difficulty. Even the best families and most loving marriages have moments of strain and conflict. But the relationships between the Father, the Son, and Holy Spirit aren't like that. The Spirit is so closely connected to the other members of the Trinity that He is sometimes called 'the Spirit of God' (Rom. 8:9, referring to God the Father) or 'the Spirit of Jesus' (Acts 16:7). As we saw in the last chapter, the Spirit was the cause of Jesus' conception in His mother's womb, and all throughout Jesus' ministry the Spirit was present to lead (Luke 4:1) Him, empower (Luke 4:14) Him, and even raise Him from the dead (Rom. 1:4). Because there is an essential unity between the three persons of the Trinity, they all love each other and delight in each other and work together to accomplish their purpose.

Take time to read these two statements that Jesus made to His disciples shortly before His death:

'But the Helper, the Holy Spirit, whom the Father will send in my name, he will teach you all things and bring to your remembrance all that I have said to you' (John 14:26).

'When the Spirit of truth comes, he will guide you into all the truth, for he will not speak on his own authority, but whatever he hears he will speak, and he will declare to you the things that are to come. He *will glorify me, for he will take what is mine and declare it to you. All that the Father has is mine; therefore I said that he will take what is mine and declare it to you'* (John 16:13–15).

WHAT DOES THE SPIRIT DO?

The Holy Spirit is sometimes called 'the shy member of the Trinity' because instead of pointing people to Himself, His work serves to honour and reveal the Father and the Son. The Father (Luke 11:13) and Son (John 16:7) send the Spirit to God's people in order to accomplish their purposes and declare their truth.

But what *are* those purposes? What does the Spirit *do*?

 ILLUSTRATION

Because He points to the glory of the Father and Son, we might be tempted to think that the Spirit is somehow less important or powerful than the other persons of the Trinity. But if you think about the strongest and most loving people that you know, they probably don't go around making much of themselves. In fact, people who are hungry for their own glory are usually pretty weak and insecure; you probably can recall someone like this pretty quickly. Instead, true greatness is found in celebrating and loving others. The Spirit's commitment to the glory of the Father and Son is not a sign of weakness; it's an indication of His greatness!

It's impossible to give a complete list of everything the Spirit does, but here are four things that will be helpful for us to know as we seek to live as faithful Christians:

1. THE SPIRIT INSPIRED THE BIBLE.

 '…knowing this first of all, that no prophecy of Scripture comes from someone's own interpretation. For no prophecy was ever produced by the will of man, but men spoke from God as they were carried along by the Holy Spirit' (2 Pet. 1:20–21).

The Bible is not merely the words, advice, memories, and opinions of human beings. Rather, the people who wrote the Bible were taught (1 Cor. 2:12–13), inspired (2 Tim. 3:16), and guided (John 16:12–13) by the Holy Spirit. For this reason, when we read the Bible, we must accept it as the Word of God to us. This means we're not free to pick and choose the bits we like and dislike because these are the words the Holy Spirit has spoken to us.

2. THE SPIRIT MAKES US CHRISTIANS.

By nature, every human being is both spiritually dead and an enemy of God (Eph. 2:1–3). This is why Jesus says we need to be born again; we need to be made spiritually alive (John 3:3). But here's the problem: we can't get spiritual life on our own. We can't *make* ourselves be born again any more than we *made* ourselves be born in the first place—any more than a dead body can *make* itself get up and walk. The solution to this problem comes through the work of the Holy Spirit. By the Spirit's power, spiritually dead people are made spiritually alive. By the Spirit's power, spiritually dead people turn from their love of sin and put their trust in Jesus.

 'It is the Spirit who gives life; the flesh is no help at all' (John 6:63).

Jesus is saying that our human nature and human strength and human wisdom cannot help when it comes to producing spiritual life. This is the work of the Spirit alone. No one can become a true follower of Christ unless the Holy Spirit first moves powerfully to give him or her spiritual life.

 SAMUEL

Samuel's life illustrates this truth well. He knows he never could have changed himself. He came from a hopeless and violent world. He had no idea it was even *possible* to live differently. Only the powerful work of the Holy Spirit could make him begin to hate his sin and love the things of God. Can you see the direction your life would have taken if God the Spirit hadn't entered the picture?

3. THE SPIRIT LIVES IN CHRISTIANS AND MAKES US HOLY.

The Holy Spirit's work doesn't end when He causes us to be spiritually born again. He doesn't just swoop in, make us alive, and then leave us alone to try and figure things out. Instead, the Spirit lives inside of Christians from the moment of salvation. His presence in our lives sets us apart as God's special possession (Rom. 8:9) and gives us assurance that we really are God's children (Rom. 8:16).

 'But the fruit of the Spirit is love, joy, peace, patience, kindness, goodness, faithfulness, gentleness, self-control; against such things there is no law' (Gal. 5:22–23).

When the Spirit lives inside us, He begins to bear good fruit in our lives. His presence and power help us grow in characteristics that please God (things like love, joy, peace, etc.).

But it's really important to realize that there's a difference between the work of the Holy Spirit in making us spiritually alive and the work the Holy Spirit does in helping up grow in holiness. When the Spirit causes us to be born again, we do nothing except *receive* that blessing. But our growth in holiness is different. Here, the Spirit is powerfully at work, but we have to work alongside Him. We can *choose* to go after the sinful desires of our flesh (Gal. 5:19–21 gives you a list of some of these things) or we can *choose* to walk in the power the Spirit gives to us. If we are to grow in holiness, we must cooperate with the Spirit's work, keeping our actions and attitudes in step with the way He's leading us.

4. THE SPIRIT WORKS IN THE CHURCH.

The Holy Spirit gives spiritual gifts to individual believers. These are special abilities or strengths that aren't required of every believer but are given in order to help build up the church. Not everyone has the same gift, and not all gifts seem extraordinary, but every Christian has *some* gift of the Spirit. We should desire these gifts so we can help our brothers and sisters in the church (1 Cor. 14:1), but the Spirit is the one who chooses how He will distribute God's gifts to God's people (1 Cor. 12:11).

These gifts created some confusion and conflict among the earliest Christians. Some seemed more impressive than others, and one group of people looked down on others whose gifts seemed less extraordinary. In response, the Apostle Paul warned Christians not to look down on each other, but to use their gifts to serve one another and strengthen the church.

'To each is given the manifestation of the Spirit for the common good. For to one is given through the Spirit the utterance of wisdom, and to another the utterance of knowledge according to the same Spirit, to another faith by the same Spirit, to another gifts of healing by the one Spirit, to another the working of miracles, to another prophecy, to another the ability to distinguish between spirits, to another various kinds of tongues, to another the interpretation of tongues. All these are empowered by one and the same Spirit, who apportions to each one individually as he wills' (1 Cor. 12:7–11).

 ILLUSTRATION

The Apostle Paul uses the image of a body to explain the role of the Spirit's gifts in the church (1 Cor. 12:14–27). Some parts of the body might seem more important and glamorous, but the body as a whole needs its individual members, the eyes and feet and hands. One part can't think it's better than another because they're all members of a whole.

A church works the same way. Every local church is a living thing made up of individuals who all have a part to play. What gift might the Spirit have given you to help you build up and serve the church?

SAMUEL

Samuel's impression of the Holy Spirit is marked by his experience of people shouting and flopping around. There's debate in Christian circles about whether some of the more spectacular gifts were only intended for the early church, but what's clear is that the Spirit *doesn't* bring disorder but peace (1 Cor. 14:33). His gifts are never meant simply to shock or excite people. Instead, they're meant to help the church grow in love and godliness. Some people in church might try to make Samuel feel like a 'second-class' Christian because he didn't experience the Spirit's presence in dramatic ways. But what Samuel should really be longing and praying for is the work of the Spirit in making him more like Christ.

MEMORY VERSE

'But the fruit of the Spirit is love, joy, peace, patience, kindness, goodness, faithfulness, gentleness, self-control; against such things there is no law' (Gal. 5:22–23).

SUMMARY

The Holy Spirit is the third person of the Trinity, fully divine in His own right. He points people to the glory of the Father and Son and gives God's people everything they need to be saved and walk in holiness. Christians must cherish the Spirit's presence and strive to walk in holiness. They must also use the gifts the Spirit has given them to serve others in the church.

WHAT'S THE POINT?

Jesus has the final word, not evil or demons.

4. SPIRIT WORLD: ANGELS AND DEMONS

RECAP

So far we've looked at the fact that the one true God exists eternally in three persons: the Father, the Son, and the Holy Spirit. We've seen how God the Son, who has existed from all eternity, entered our world by taking on human flesh in order to save us. And we've seen how God the Spirit, a fully divine person in His own right, works in us to save us and glorify the Father and Son.

Now we turn to the subject of angels and demons.

SAMUEL

When Samuel was a teenager, he once accidentally found himself on the turf of a rival gang. Turning a corner, he saw a group of young men coming toward him, and he was sure he was about to be in big trouble. But suddenly, the rival gang turned around and Samuel was able to find his way home safely. When he told his mother what happened, she was sure Samuel's 'guardian angel' had been looking out for him.

Is this the kind of thing angels do?

Maybe the easiest way to approach this subject is to ask and answer a few basic questions.

WHAT ARE ANGELS?

Angels are *spiritual beings created by God.* They're 'spiritual beings' (Heb. 1:14), meaning that they don't have physical bodies. This is why they're normally invisible to us, though God does sometimes choose to reveal their presence (check out 2 Kings 6:11–19 for a cool story about someone being made able to see the Lord's angels who were around him).

That being said, angels aren't eternal beings. They were created by God in the past for His own purposes. The Bible seems to indicate that there are different kinds of angels or heavenly beings. Some are called 'the seraphim' and 'the cherubim,' and some have a higher rank than others (an angel named Michael is referred to as an 'archangel'). But we're not given much detail about what makes one kind of angel different from another.

WHAT DO ANGELS DO?

Angels act as powerful servants of God. In the Bible, angels

carry messages to people (Luke 1:26–38)

bring God's judgment in certain situations (2 Sam. 24:16–17, Acts 12:23)

serve as warriors in the heavenly army (Rev. 12:7–8)

declare God's praises (Job 38:7, Ps. 103:20)

rejoice in the way He has acted to save human beings (Luke 15:10, Rev. 5:11–12).

'For he will command his angels concerning you to guard you in all your ways. On their hands they will bear you up, lest you strike your foot against a stone' (Ps. 91:11–12).

In this Psalm, we see that one of the ways God cares for His people is by sending His invisible (to us!) angels to guard them. Samuel's mother might be correct that an angel helped him out of this dangerous situation. Perhaps you've had experiences where it seemed you had some assistance from an unseen helper. All of this might be the case, but there's little in the Bible to make us think we *all* have an individual angel who's been assigned as our 'guardian angel.' Instead, we should trust that God watches over us and sends His servants to help us when we need it.

HOW SHOULD WE RELATE TO ANGELS?

The Bible tells us that we may sometimes encounter disguised angels in our daily lives: *'Do not neglect to show hospitality to strangers, for thereby some have entertained angels unawares'* (Heb. 13:2, see Gen. 18:1–15 for an example). While that should make us eager to care for strangers, the Bible doesn't give us any encouragement to spend our time looking for encounters with angels.

It's true that angels are real and at work in our world, but when they appear to humans in the Bible, it's always at God's command, not because people have sought them.

We pray to God our Father, never to angels.

We worship God, never angels (Col. 2:18, Rev. 19:10).

We should be grateful to God for the ways He sends His angels to care for us, but we shouldn't become obsessed with them to the point where we neglect our duty to love and obey God Himself.

WHAT ARE DEMONS? WHO IS SATAN?

Jesus often encountered demons in the course of His ministry (for example, see Luke 8:26–37), but the Gospel writers don't really explain what they are. They seem to assume we know. Thankfully, we have some information later in the New Testament that helps us fill in some gaps in our knowledge. In 2 Peter, the Apostle Peter writes about angels who sinned:

'God did not spare angels when they sinned, but cast them into hell and committed them to chains of gloomy darkness to be kept until the judgment' (2 Pet. 2:4).

And in the book of Jude, we read:

'And the angels who did not stay within their own position of authority, but left their proper dwelling, he has kept in eternal chains under gloomy darkness until the judgment of the great day' (Jude 6).

From these verses, we can say **demons are angels who were once in heaven ('their proper dwelling'), but they sinned against God** by not staying 'within their own position of authority.' We're not told exactly what this means, but it seems demons rebelled against the status God had given them. As a result, this group was cast into hell, where they await final judgment.

Satan is merely a fallen angel, the leader of the demons. His name means 'adversary,' and he is committed to opposing God and His people at every turn.

Satan and his demons are powerful creatures, but they're not without limits. They sometimes torment people in groups (see Luke 8:2 for an example), which wouldn't be necessary if each demon was all-powerful. In fact, it seems that some demons are more or less wicked and destructive than others (Matt. 12:45). Demons cannot be in all places at all times, but they're creatures that must come and go (see James 4:7 and Luke 4:13). Demons don't know everything, for only God knows what will happen in the future (Isa. 46:9–10) and searches our hearts and minds (Rev. 2:23).

WHAT DO DEMONS DO?

The Bible shows us that Satan and other demons are hard at work in the world. Specifically, they look to create and encourage:

- *Physical pain and suffering* – Demons are often causing physical disability and agony in humans. They seem to delight in this (for example: Matt. 12:22).

- *Confusion and mental turmoil* – When demons are active, people sometimes lose their capacity to behave in a rational and controlled way (for example: Mark 5:1–13).

- *False worship* – The idols and false gods that the people of Canaan worshipped were in fact demons (see Deut. 32:17). When people worshipped them, they were actually worshipping Satan and his demons.

- *Sin in God's people* – We see Satan tempting God's people to disobey Him (see 1 Chron. 21:1 and Luke 22:31). The devil schemes against them (Eph. 6:11) in order to trip them up spiritually.

In order to accomplish these goals, we see demons executing the following strategies:

- *Attack* – The Bible shows us people who are especially affected by the power and influence of demons (we might say they 'have a demon' or are 'possessed'). Ephesians 6:16 even speaks of 'the flaming darts of the evil one,' which seems to indicate that believers should expect to experience regular spiritual attacks from demonic forces.

- *Deceit* – The Lord Jesus said this about the devil: '*When he lies, he speaks out of his own character, for he is a liar and the father of lies*' (John 8:44). Demonic forces tempt people to disbelieve

God and blind unbelievers to the beauty and truth of God's salvation in Christ (2 Cor. 4:4). If Satan were honest about his intentions, very few people would follow him. Instead, he pretends to be an angel of light in order to deceive many (2 Cor. 11:13–15).

- *Temptation* – Satan lures people into sin by encouraging them to act on their foolish thoughts (Gen. 3:4–6), excessive desires (1 Cor. 7:5), and sinful tendencies (Acts 5:3).

SAMUEL

Lately, Samuel has been struggling with depression; he's even thought about taking his life. His aunt tells him that he may have a demonic 'stronghold' in his life that would explain why he is so often upset and unhappy. Are Samuel's problems his fault, or can they be blamed on the activity of demons? How can he know? In any case, what should he do about it?

ARE DEMONS RESPONSIBLE FOR MY ACTIONS?

The Bible doesn't spend very much time talking about demonic activity as it relates to our sin. Instead, we see that

the source of our evil deeds is often our own hearts (Matt. 15:19)

> *out of which flows our words (James 3:5–6)*

> > *and our deeds (Gal. 5:19–21).*

Basically, we're pretty good at doing what's wrong; we don't need a lot of demonic influence in order to sin.

And yet, we *do* need to be careful as we think about how demons are involved in our lives. There's great danger in being completely unaware of the unseen forces that seek to do us serious spiritual harm. We must resist the devil (James 4:7) and pray vigorously against his influence in both our lives and the world around us (Matt. 6:13). The Apostle Peter warns Christians:

'Be sober-minded; be watchful. Your adversary the devil prowls around like a roaring lion, seeking someone to devour' (1 Pet. 5:8).

But on the other hand, we shouldn't go around expecting to find a demon lurking behind every problem and every instance of suffering. The Bible doesn't assume that every experience of illness, addiction, and failure is the direct result of demonic activity. Sometimes, *we* are the problem. We do things we know are wrong, we give in to our own sinful desires, and we make foolish choices.

This is why God's Word doesn't tell people ensnared in sin to go around casting out the demons that are causing problems, but rather to do far more 'boring' things like flee youthful passions (2 Tim. 2:22), resist the devil (1 Pet. 5:9), and confess their sins to one another (James 5:16).

'And you, who were dead in your trespasses and the uncircumcision of your flesh, God made alive together with him, having forgiven us all our trespasses, by cancelling the record of debt that stood against us with its legal demands. This he set aside, nailing it to the cross. He disarmed the rulers and authorities and put them to open shame, by triumphing over them in him' (Col. 2:13–15).

In the end, the most important thing to know about Satan and his demons is that Jesus has conquered them through His life, death, and resurrection! Now, when Paul talks about 'the rulers and authorities' in this passage, he is referring to the devil and his demons (see Eph. 6:12 for something similar). When Jesus died on the cross, He scored a decisive victory over the forces that oppose God and His people. Those forces are now disarmed because Jesus has taken away everything they can use against us.

When Satan accuses God's people of sin, he finds that our sin and guilt have already been paid for; they've been nailed to the cross of Christ.

> **Ultimately, then, there's no force in the world—no matter how powerful, no matter how evil—that can separate one of God's children from His love (Rom. 8:38–39).**

MEMORY VERSE

'Little children, you are from God and have overcome them, for he who is in you is greater than he who is in the world' (1 John 4:4).

SUMMARY

Angels and demons are real spiritual beings at work in the world around us. We should be both thankful to God for the ways He uses His angels to care for us and also on guard against the ways demonic forces seek to do us spiritual harm. However, Scripture doesn't encourage us to focus and speculate endlessly about these matters. Instead, we should focus our energy on serving God and living in light of what Jesus has done for us through His death and resurrection.

WHAT'S THE POINT?

The Bible helps us understand what has gone wrong in the world.

5. CREATION AND FALL

So far we've focused on things that are largely invisible to us: the Trinity, angels, and demons. We can't touch or taste or see these things, but they're very real and they have a very real impact on our world.

 SAMUEL

If you looked at the story of Samuel's life, it would be hard to understand. How can he be a basically nice, caring, and generous person... but also capable of doing terrible things, especially in his past? Samuel has long wondered about his friends from the gang. In most circumstances, they were loyal and loving, but they also did terrible things to people. To varying degrees, this moral contrast is true of everyone. We all seem to be a mix of good and bad, kindness and selfishness. Even the best people have faults; even the worst people usually have some decent qualities. How do we explain this reality?

WHO MADE ALL OF THIS?

If we want to understand the world we live in, it's best to start at the beginning. And so it's not surprising the very first thing the Bible addresses is the question of where we come from.

 'In the beginning, God created the heavens and the earth' (Gen. 1:1).

That might seem like a simple statement, but there's important information packed in there:

+ We see **the world has a beginning.** That is to say, it hasn't always been. There was a time when there were no heavens and no earth.

+ But we also see that before the beginning, God was already there. **God has no beginning; He has always been.**

+ Finally, we see **it was God who made the heavens and the earth.** Things didn't come into existence through purely natural forces; nothing 'just happened.' God made an entire universe simply by speaking things into existence. Genesis 1:3 tells us: 'God said, "Let there be light," and there was light.'

If our world 'just happened,' if it created itself through a massive explosion or a slow development over time, then it's hard to see how it has any purpose or meaning.

> *What does it mean to say things are 'right' or 'wrong' if everything that exists is just an accident?*

> *How can we say something is 'good' or 'bad' if we're nothing more than the product of chemicals and energy?*

But that's not the world we live in. The God who created this world is personal; He knows us and can be known by us. Because He made everything (including us!) **He has authority over everything** (including us!). He gets to say what's right and wrong. 'Authority' is the right to make the rules, and God the Creator makes the rules for His universe. He tells us how to live. He tells us what is good and what is bad, and He doesn't need our advice or input. Furthermore, we don't get to question the decisions God makes or argue with Him about His actions. For example, look at the tongue-lashing Job gets in Job 38–41 when he tries to demand that God explain Himself!

The fact that God created the world also means everything tells us important things about the One who made them. Just like a painting or a sculpture reveals something of the creativity and vision of the artist, so the world God made shows us something of what He is like. The Apostle Paul tells us that every human being is aware of God's existence, because He has shown Himself to us in the things He has made:

'For what can be known about God is plain to them, because God has shown it to them. For his invisible attributes, namely, his eternal power and divine nature, have been clearly perceived, ever since the creation of the world, in the things that have been made. So they are without excuse' (Rom. 1:19–20).

And King David writes in the Psalms:

'The heavens declare the glory of God, and the sky above proclaims his handiwork' (Ps. 19:1).

Just by looking at the world God has made, we can understand all sorts of things about His 'divine nature.' His

glory,

   power,

      beauty,

         creativity,

           justice, and

           strength

are all on display in His creation.

STOP

Does the fact that God created everything mean the world has a purpose? If everything just began to exist on its own, would it be possible for the world to have ultimate meaning and purpose?

IN THE IMAGE

The book of Genesis tells us that God made the world over the course of six days (He rested from His work of creation on the seventh day). On each day, of creation, God made something new. For example, on the third day He made all sorts of plants and trees, and on the sixth day God made the first human beings: Adam (the first man) and Eve (the first woman). Together, they were the high point of God's work.

 'Then God said, "Let us make man in our image, after our likeness. And let them have dominion over the fish of the sea and over the birds of the heavens and over the livestock and over all the earth and over every creeping thing that creeps on the earth." So God created man in his own image, in the image of God he created him; male and female he created them. And God blessed them. And God said to them, "Be fruitful and multiply and fill the earth and subdue it, and have dominion over the fish of the sea and over the birds of the heavens and over every living thing that moves on the earth" (Gen. 1:26–28).

Notice what we learn about human beings from these verses:

+ Human beings **were made male and female**. Gender was God's idea from the beginning.

+ Human beings were given **'dominion' over the world**. In other words, they are supposed to act as God's agents on the earth. They do this as they fill the earth with more humans, all of whom would care for and rule over the animals, plants, and the rest of creation.

+ Human beings were **made in God's image**. More than any other part of creation, men and women are designed to demonstrate what God is like. People are capable of having rational thoughts, forming personal relationships, creating works of beauty, and making moral decisions. In these ways (and others), they reflect something of God's goodness and character.

> **STOP**
>
> Every human being you've ever met or ever will meet has been created in God's image. How does this shape the way you think about the value of human life? How should this change the way you treat others on a day-to-day basis?

 'No human being can tame the tongue. It is a restless evil, full of deadly poison. With it we bless our Lord and Father, and with it we curse people who are made in the likeness of God' (James 3:8–9).

A DEVASTATING FALL

After creating Adam and Eve, God declared all that He had made 'very good' (Gen. 1:31). But it wasn't long before things went from good to bad. You see, God had told Adam and Eve they were free to eat *anything* they wanted in the world that God had created—with one exception. They were not to eat from the tree of the knowledge of good and evil. As long as they obeyed God's commandment, they'd live forever in perfect happiness. But if they disobeyed God and ate from that tree, they would 'surely die' (Gen. 2:17).

You probably know how the rest of the story goes. The devil shows up in the Garden in the form of a serpent, and he tempts Eve. The results are disastrous:

'He said to the woman, "Did God actually say, 'You shall not eat of any tree in the garden'?" And the woman said to the serpent, "We

may eat of the fruit of the trees in the garden, but God said, 'You shall not eat of the fruit of the tree that is in the midst of the garden, neither shall you touch it, lest you die.'" But the serpent said to the woman, "You will not surely die. For God knows that when you eat of it your eyes will be opened, and you will be like God, knowing good and evil." So when the woman saw that the tree was good for food, and that it was a delight to the eyes, and that the tree was to be desired to make one wise, she took of its fruit and ate, and she also gave some to her husband who was with her, and he ate' (Gen. 3:1–6).

Did you notice what lay at the heart of the devil's temptation? He questioned whether or not Adam and Eve ought to believe and obey the words of God. He suggests that God didn't really mean what He said, and if He did, they shouldn't believe Him. Eve (and Adam after her) decided not to believe and not to obey God— and so sin entered into the world. Sometimes, Christians refer to this as 'the Fall' because when Adam and Eve sinned, mankind 'fell' from perfection into a state of sinfulness.

SAMUEL

It seems like there are a million different voices in Samuel's ear. The people around him all have opinions about how he should live his life. His old friends seem happy with their lives full of drinking and drugs and sleeping around. His family seems to live for nothing other than financial security. And then God's Word has a completely different vision of how he should live. How does he know whose 'voice' to trust? As we will see, all of our problems began when someone listened to a voice other than God's.

CONSEQUENCES

Adam and Eve's sin had dire consequences, not just for themselves but for all of humanity that followed after them. A few of them include:

+ **Sin** – all of Adam's descendants (that's you and me and everyone else) are born with an inherited sinful nature. We all sin because we're all sinners; the sinful things we do arise out of our sinful hearts.

+ **Death** – God promised that disobedience would bring death, and that's exactly what happened. When Adam and Eve sinned, physical death entered the world. But even more than that, 'spiritual death' became a reality. We're spiritually dead (Eph. 2:1) and deserve eternal punishment for our rebellion against God.

+ **Curse** – because of sin, all of creation has been placed under a curse (Gen. 3:16–19, Rom. 8:20–22). The world doesn't work the way that it should. Natural disasters, famine, futility, suffering, and pain are all a result of sin.

 ILLUSTRATION

Have you ever seen a funhouse mirror? If you look into a mirror that's been curved inward, you'll see your reflection but it will seem comically short and fat. If you look in a mirror that has been curved outward, it will still be your reflection, but it will be ridiculously tall and thin. Maybe that's a helpful way to think about what it means for people to be 'fallen' but still made in God's image. We still reflect what God is like, but instead of being clear and sharp the image is badly distorted. This is why the same person can be capable of love and hatred, kindness and cruelty.

 MEMORY VERSE

'For all have sinned and fall short of the glory of God' (Rom. 3:23).

 SUMMARY

God is the creator of everything, and as a result He has authority over the world and everyone who lives in it. He created Adam and Eve to reflect His image as they cared for the world, but they weren't content to believe His word and obey His commands. So they disbelieved and disobeyed God. As a result, all people are sinners, estranged from God and under His righteous judgment.

WHAT'S THE POINT?

Jesus' death on the cross is an amazing gift.

6. ATONEMENT AND ELECTION

RECAP

The Bible teaches us that God made all humans in His image. As a result, all people have dignity and the capacity for love, beauty, and creativity. But because of sin, we're all separated from God and spiritually dead. How can we possibly reconcile ourselves to God if we have made ourselves His enemies? How can spiritually dead people come back to life?

SAMUEL

All his life, Samuel has been surrounded by images of Jesus' cross. Huge wooden crosses loomed over him from the tops of churches in his hometown. Priests wore crosses with Jesus hanging on them around their necks. Gang members had large crosses tattooed on their backs. Elderly aunts were always crossing themselves with their hands whenever something important was happening. But he never understood the meaning of the cross and why it was that Jesus had to die that way.

HOW JESUS' DEATH SAVES US

We cannot fix our sin situation because *we're the problem, not the solution!* If things are ever going to be made right, God is going to have to be the one who does it. Thankfully, that's exactly what He did for us by sending His Son.

'For all have sinned and fall short of the glory of God, and are justified by his grace as a gift, through the redemption that is in Christ Jesus, whom God put forward as a propitiation by his blood, to be received by faith. This was to show God's righteousness, because in his divine forbearance he had passed over former sins. It was to show his righteousness at the present time, so that he might be just and the justifier of the one who has faith in Jesus' (Rom. 3:23–26).

The first time you read it, this passage from the Apostle Paul might seem hard to understand. After all, it's full of words we don't use very often. But if we pull it apart, we see that it tells us exactly how Jesus' death saves us:

+ Paul reminds us that all of us have **sinned**. We thought about that a lot in the last chapter. This is the problem we need God to solve for us.

+ Though we have sinned, we can be **justified**. To be justified is to be accepted as someone who is righteous. And yet, it's more than just being found 'not guilty'; it's being declared to be good.

+ The only way for us to be justified is by God's **grace as a gift**. We cannot make ourselves righteous because even if we stopped sinning right now (which isn't going to happen!), we still have committed plenty of sins in the past. We need God to be gracious, to give sinners a right standing before God as a gift we do not deserve.

+ This gift comes to us through the **redemption that is in Christ Jesus**. That is to say, it's only through Jesus that God delivers us from our sin problem.

+ The way God did this was by putting Jesus forward as a **propitiation**. That's a complicated (but important) way of saying 'something that satisfies wrath.' God was rightly angry at our sin, but Jesus made it so that we were reconciled to God. Now, because of Jesus' perfect sacrifice, God is pleased with us.

+ The way Jesus did this was **by His blood**. Here, Paul is talking about Jesus' death on the cross. On the cross, Jesus satisfied the anger of God against all the sins of everyone who would ever trust in Him. God poured out His righteous justice on Jesus, so now there is nothing but love and grace left for us.

+ We receive this amazing gift **through faith**. It's obvious that we cannot add anything to what Jesus has done. All we can do is accept God's gift by trusting in Jesus for our salvation.

+ In this way, God shows He is **just and the justifier of the one who has faith in Jesus**. He is just because He didn't just wave a magic wand and pretend that our sins went away. If God did that, He wouldn't be a just God; after all, what kind of judge lets guilty people go free? In order to set us free, He had to do something about our guilt. And so instead of simply ignoring our sin, God sent His Son to satisfy the demands of justice against our sins by dying on the cross. By punishing Jesus for our sins, God demonstrates that He is just. He is also our justifier because He set in motion this entire plan to provide for our forgiveness and restoration through Jesus.

Jesus' death on the cross wasn't simply a magnificent gesture of love. It wasn't just a way to show us how we ought to sacrifice for each other. When Jesus died on the cross, He actually accomplished something. He atoned for (that is, He made up for) our sins by stepping into our place, taking our punishment, and then rising from the dead in victory.

STOP

Lots of people think the different religions of the world offer equally valid ways for people to be right with God. Does the death of Jesus change how we think about that idea? If there *were* other ways for people to be saved from their sins, why would Jesus choose to die like that? If there was another way to be saved, would Jesus have died at all?

A GREAT EXCHANGE

'For our sake he made him to be sin who knew no sin, so that in him we might become the righteousness of God' (2 Cor. 5:21).

A right relationship with God requires us not only to be free from sin. We also must have righteousness. To put it simply: it's not enough for us just to be 'not bad'; we also need to be good. As a result, sinful people have two basic problems: a **sin problem** and a **righteousness problem**.

+ Our **sin problem** is that we are guilty of doing, thinking, and loving all kinds of bad things.

+ Our **righteousness problem** is that we lack moral goodness; we haven't lived holy and blameless lives.

Jesus had neither of those problems, which means He is able to save us. Because He had no sin of His own, Jesus did not deserve to die. As He gave up His life on the cross, He did not experience the anger of God at His sins (because He did not have any). Instead, He was able to take our sin on Himself. As Paul says in 2 Corinthians 5:21, Jesus was 'made to be sin' for our sake. And because He was perfectly obedient to His heavenly Father, He can give us His righteousness as a gift.

Let me state this as simply as I can: whenever you come to Jesus in faith, God the Father counts Jesus' holiness as yours. His righteousness is credited to you *as if it were yours*. In this way, we 'become the righteousness of God,' but only because of Jesus.

ILLUSTRATION

Imagine that you're taking an important test in school, but you're not a very good student. You know that passing the exam means more than just not getting questions wrong—you need to answer the questions correctly! Unfortunately, when the results come back, you find that you missed almost every question.

But wait: imagine now that the smartest kid in your class offers to take your bad grade (and the consequences that come with it) *and* the teacher agrees to give you his perfect score. It's not a perfect comparison, but this gives us some sense of what Jesus did for us. Despite our failure, Jesus' perfection is credited to us through faith in Him.

CHOSEN IN LOVE

With everything we've seen so far, there are some questions we have to ask:

> *If every human being is the same in terms of being spiritually dead in their sins, why is it that some people become followers of Jesus but most people don't?*

> *Why does someone like Samuel find salvation and deliverance from his life of sin, while so many of his friends and family don't?*

> *Is there something special about Samuel?*

> *Was he less spiritually dead than others?*

> *Was he smarter or more spiritually sensitive?*

The Bible answers these questions. It explains why it is that people become followers of Jesus, and it has nothing to do with anything good in us.

 'Blessed be the God and Father of our Lord Jesus Christ, who has blessed us in Christ with every spiritual blessing in the heavenly places, even as he chose us in him before the foundation of the world, that we should be holy and blameless before him. In love he predestined us for adoption to himself as sons through Jesus Christ, according to the purpose of his will.... In him we have obtained an inheritance, having been predestined according to the purpose of him who works all things according to the counsel of his will.' (Eph. 1:3–5, 11).

In these verses Paul tells us that God chose each one of His people for salvation 'before the foundation of the world.' This choice by God regarding who will be saved is referred to as 'election.' In electing (or choosing) His people, God sets His love on them and draws them to believe in Jesus and be saved (John 6:44).

So, when we ask why some people believe in Jesus and some people don't, the most important answer is that the only way people are able to believe in Jesus is if God the Father has already chosen them to believe.

+ The Bible teaches us that God's election is **unconditional**. In other words, God doesn't choose people based on anything good He saw in them. This is important to understand—and Paul makes a big deal about it in Romans 9:10–13—because it means our salvation highlights God's kindness and not our worthiness.

+ God's election is also *free*, because the choice is His alone. God told Moses that He was free to show mercy and compassion to anyone He wanted (Exod. 33:19). Similarly, Paul tells us that God is free to harden the heart of anyone He wishes to

(Rom. 9:18). No one *made* God elect people for salvation, and in fact Paul tells us that He did it for His own reasons ('according to the counsel of his will') and for His own glory (Rom. 9:23).

+ Election also means **we cannot lose our salvation.** If God chose us (instead of our choosing Him), who can possibly undo His choice (see John 10:27–29)? Anyone who is truly a follower of Jesus will be kept by God's incredible love until the end.

We might be tempted to think election is unfair. How can God hold people accountable for the fact that *He* didn't choose *them*? But we must remember that we have all freely rebelled against God and earned our condemnation. There's no one who longs to believe in Jesus and wants to be reconciled to God who is being kept from doing so. Whether we reject God or embrace His salvation through Jesus, we all do the things we genuinely want to do. When Paul answers this objection, he reminds us that in the end we don't have the right to question God's ways (Rom. 9:19–24).

The big take-away here is that God has freely chosen a group of people to be the recipients of His special, saving love. These people receive God's great mercy through Christ. We cannot understand why God chooses some people and not others; we can only be certain that God is always good and right in all that He does.

 MEMORY VERSE

'What then shall we say to these things? If God is for us, who can be against us? He who did not spare his own Son but gave him up for us all, how will he not also with him graciously give us all things? Who shall bring any charge against God's elect? It is God who justifies' (Rom. 8:31–33).

SUMMARY

In love, God chose some hopeless sinners to receive His amazing love. Jesus took the guilt and condemnation of all these people on Himself when He hung on the cross; Jesus' triumph became clear when God raised Jesus from the dead. Now, everyone who trusts in Jesus receives His righteousness as a gift and is considered by God the Father to be completely righteous.

WHAT'S THE POINT?

With GOD's help, we must deal with our sins.

7. SANCTIFICATION AND PERSEVERANCE

In our last chapter, we looked at what God has done for us in Christ. When we were still trapped in our sins and guilt, God sent His Son to save us. Jesus lived a life of perfect obedience to His heavenly Father, took our punishment on the cross, and rose from the dead in victory over sin and death. The Holy Spirit grants new spiritual life to everyone chosen by the Father, giving us the gift of repentance and faith in Jesus.

Simply put, it couldn't be clearer that salvation is God's work, not ours. But that doesn't mean there's *nothing* for us to do as we live as Christians.

 SAMUEL

Once Samuel trusted in Christ, he noticed some immediate changes in his life. He found himself thinking about how to please Jesus with his life. He wasn't losing his temper as much and he showed more patience with his family. When he saw someone in need, he now felt a newfound desire to help. But there were also some things he was trying to change that didn't seem to change quickly. He felt guilty about how often he lied in order to cover up the wrong things he did. But stopping was difficult. There were also times he found it really hard to turn down opportunities to hook up with girls. If he's honest, he's a bit disappointed God hasn't taken away some of these struggles with sin.

YOU MUST BE HOLY

Christians should be holy. They should strive to please God with their thoughts, attitudes, emotions, and actions. Now, the word 'holy' might sound a bit old-fashioned, but **holiness is a very real, very practical, and very important issue** for people who would be followers of Jesus.

 'Strive for peace with everyone, and for the holiness without which no one will see the Lord' (Heb. 12:14).

The author of Hebrews is clear: without holiness, we have no hope of seeing God in heaven. A Christian's holiness clarifies the difference between people who still belong to the devil and people who have been adopted into God's family through Christ (1 John 3:10).

YOU HAVE BEEN MADE GOOD

Now, that might sound scary to you. After all, we've seen pretty clearly that none of us can be good enough to please God. We might be able to keep our external actions under control, but none of us can claim to have holy attitudes, thoughts, and emotions.

> *So, if we must have holiness in order to see God, are we all hopeless?*

Not at all! As we've seen, when we come to Jesus we receive His righteousness as a free gift. So anyone who is in Christ has all of the holiness he or she needs in order to be admitted into heaven. This is why the authors of the New Testament write to normal Christians and call them 'saints' (a word that means 'holy ones'). For example, at the beginning of his 1 Corinthians, Paul greets the Christians:

'To the church of God that is in Corinth, to those sanctified in Christ Jesus, called to be saints together with all those who in every place call

upon the name of our Lord Jesus Christ, both their Lord and ours' (1 Cor. 1:2).

Now, as the rest of the letter makes clear, these Christians had serious issues. They were fighting with each other, taking each other to court, getting drunk at the Lord's Supper, and tolerating some nasty sexual immorality. They weren't perfect, but because they were united to Christ by faith they—and you!—have His perfect holiness credited to them. They were 'sanctified in Christ Jesus.' All Christians are holy before the Lord because of the work of Jesus.

NOW, BE GOOD

So all Christians are counted as righteous in Christ. But that's not the end of the story. Jesus didn't die only to forgive us for our sins; He also died so that we could be freed from sin's power over us. It's as if God is saying to His people: 'In Jesus, you've been made holy. Now go out into the world and be what you already are!'

The holiness of Jesus should increasingly be visible in our actions, attitudes, words, decisions, and thoughts. We must never think our growth in goodness *makes* God love us. Instead, because we know God *does* love us, we should expect to see real growth in godliness as we continue to walk with Christ.

 'For this is the will of God, your sanctification: that you abstain from sexual immorality; that each one of you know how to control his own body in holiness and honor, not in the passion of lust like the Gentiles who do not know God…. For God has not called us for impurity, but in holiness' (1 Thess. 4:3–5, 7).

You might wonder about God's plan for your life. Well, according to Paul's letter to the Thessalonians, it has less to do with where you live and what kind of work you do and more to do with 'your sanctification.' Obviously, none of us will ever be perfect until we are with Jesus in heaven. We'll always need to depend on God's forgiveness when we sin (1 John 1:8–10), but our lives should be characterized by increased Christ-likeness and freedom from sin.

 ILLUSTRATION

Holiness can seem like the 'bad news' of Christianity. Yeah, it's great that you get to go to heaven, but you have to give up all of the things that make life really fun and exciting. When God calls His people to be holy, it might seem like He's putting a container of delicious cookies on the top shelf, out of their reach.

But we misunderstand how terrible sin really is. Sin prevents us from being with God in heaven, but it also makes life in this world terrible. Of course, there are short-term pleasures that come with sin. But in the long run the payout is awful—addictions, meaninglessness, broken families, hopelessness, violence, oppression, and a host of other evils. *Sin is like a sugar-coated poison pill; it tastes sweet in the moment, but it will kill you.*

When God calls us to be holy, He isn't keeping us from cookies. He's keeping us from poison.

STOP

What would you think if someone said he was a follower of Jesus but he hadn't even tried to turn away from the sinful things in his life?

GOD'S WORK AND OURS

If holiness is so important, how do we get it? Well, our growth in holiness is different from our justification (how we are made right with God through Jesus). We don't contribute anything to our justification; from beginning to end, it's all God's work. He elected us, sent His Son, gave us new life by His Spirit, and gave us faith as a free gift. We brought nothing to that process except the sin that caused our condemnation.

But our growth in holiness is different. Consider these verses.

'Therefore, my beloved, as you have always obeyed, so now, not only as in my presence but much more in my absence, work out your own salvation with fear and trembling, for it is God who works in you, both to will and to work for his good pleasure' (Phil. 2:12–13).

This passage tells us that God is at work in us, helping us to be holy. Because of God, we want to be holy ('to will') and we actually put effort into trying to do what pleases Him ('work for his good pleasure'). But the ways God is at work in our lives doesn't mean there's nothing for us to do. We are to 'work out our salvation' humbly and respectfully; we're supposed to flesh out in our lives the salvation that Jesus has given us. Because God is at work to change us, we work hard both to do the things God calls us to do and to avoid the things He forbids.

There's no magical formula for this, but with the Holy Spirit's help we can do some of the following things:

+ **Pray** – one of the best things we can do is go to God and ask Him for the help we need to grow in holiness. That's a prayer He is always happy to answer!

+ **Read the Bible** – the Word of God is food for our souls. You will need to eat a good 'meal' if you want to fight this battle with endurance.

+ **Confess sin** – sin flourishes in the darkness. By being open with other Christians about our struggles, we shine a bright light on our sin and fight it head-on.

+ **Be in fellowship** – we're not meant to follow Jesus alone. God has given us other believers in the church to teach us, help us to say no to sin, and give us opportunities to serve and to love.

- **Flee temptation** – as long as we're alive, we'll have to battle against the sinful desires within us. That battle will be easier if we learn to avoid the people and situations that tempt us.

- **Pursue godliness** – we don't want to fall into the trap of merely trying to avoid sinful activities. We also want to grow in the things that please the Lord—things like love, service, self-control, and humility.

KEEP GOING!

You will follow Jesus for the rest of your life. The author of Hebrews warns us to continue on in the faith and not 'fall away':

'Take care, brothers, lest there be in any of you an evil, unbelieving heart, leading you to fall away from the living God. But exhort one another every day, as long as it is called "today," that none of you may be hardened by the deceitfulness of sin. For we have come to share in Christ, if indeed we hold our original confidence firm to the end' (Heb. 3:12–14).

It's clear from this passage that we're not supposed to merely follow Jesus at one point in our life. Instead, we must continue on in the faith 'to the end' and not 'fall away.' To be sure, there will be many obstacles in our path (see Luke 8:5–15), but a true follower of Christ will keep on walking with Jesus.

> *If we walk away from Jesus and never come back, that's simply evidence to prove our faith was never real in the first place (1 John 2:19).*

That might sound scary, as if we could lose our salvation. And it's true these warnings in Scripture are meant to grab our attention so that we'll not go back to our old lives before Christ. But no true follower of Jesus can ever finally fall away from Him. Like our growth in holiness, our perseverance in the faith is both our work and God's. And God promises to make sure that we make it all the way to the end.

Hear the words of Jesus:

'My sheep hear my voice, and I know them, and they follow me. I give them eternal life, and they will never perish, and no one will snatch them out of my hand. My Father, who has given them to me, is greater than all, and no one is able to snatch them out of the Father's hand' (John 10:27–29).

SAMUEL

Despite everything, there are times when Samuel feels tempted to go back to his old way of life. It felt comfortable and familiar, and following Jesus sometimes makes him feel alone and foolish. What would you tell him if he asked you what he should do?

MEMORY VERSES

'Therefore, since we are surrounded by so great a cloud of witnesses, let us also lay aside every weight, and sin which clings so closely, and let us run with endurance the race that is set before us, looking to Jesus, the founder and perfecter of our faith, who for the joy that was set before him endured the cross, despising the shame, and is seated at the right hand of the throne of God' (Heb. 12:1–2).

SUMMARY

True Christians will grow in holiness and persevere in their faith. That requires discipline and effort from us. But ultimately, we depend on God to strengthen us for the work.

WHAT'S THE POINT?

What happens in the end matters now.

8. HEAVEN AND HELL

In our last chapter we discussed the need for holiness and endurance in our walk with Jesus. Both of those things require us to work, even as we depend on God's help to help us grow and persevere. Now let's turn our attention to what awaits all of humanity at the end of their lives: either heaven or hell.

 SAMUEL

After he became involved in crime, Samuel would often worry that he was going to wind up going to hell. One of his friends in the gang used to say, 'We're going to hell, but we'll have the best stories to tell.' Samuel never laughed, because to him hell seemed terrifying. Now that he was a Christian, he no longer worried about being damned. But if he was honest, he wasn't really looking forward to heaven. He didn't really understand what made heaven so great or what it would be like to be there.

JUDGMENT

Back in our first chapter, we briefly discussed the fact that God is our holy judge. The Bible teaches that after we die—or after Jesus returns, whichever comes first—we'll face God's judgment. Here are a few places where we see this taught:

- The Apostle Paul spoke to the people of Athens and told them: *'The times of ignorance God overlooked, but now he commands all people everywhere to repent, because he has fixed a day on which he will judge the world in righteousness by a man whom he has appointed; and of this he has given assurance to all by raising him from the dead'* (Acts 17:30–31).

- The author of Hebrews writes: *'It is appointed for man to die once, and after that comes judgment'* (Heb. 9:27).

- And in 2 Corinthians, Paul tells the church: *'For we must all appear before the judgment seat of Christ, so that each one may receive what is due for what he has done in the body, whether good or evil'* (2 Cor. 5:10).

God's judgment is completely fair and just because God alone has access to every thought, deed, and attitude. *Unlike human judges, God is unbiased and never makes a mistake.* He sees everything with perfect clarity, and so His judgment is always just (Rev. 19:2).

- *'For God will bring every deed into judgment, with every secret thing, whether good or evil'* (Eccles. 12:14).

- *'And no creature is hidden from his sight, but all are naked and exposed to the eyes of him to whom we must give account'* (Heb. 4:13).

- *'For his eyes are on the ways of a man, and he sees all his steps'* (Job 34:21).

- *'The eyes of the LORD are in every place, keeping watch on the evil and the good'* (Prov. 15:3).

 'When the Son of Man comes in his glory, and all the angels with him, then he will sit on his glorious throne. Before him will be gathered

all the nations, and he will separate people one from another as a shepherd separates the sheep from the goats. And he will place the sheep on his right, but the goats on the left. Then the King will say to those on his right, "Come, you who are blessed by my Father, inherit the kingdom prepared for you from the foundation of the world"…. Then he will say to those on his left, "Depart from me, you cursed, into the eternal fire prepared for the devil and his angels"…. And these will go away into eternal punishment, but the righteous into eternal life' (Matt. 25:31–34, 41, 46).

It's hard to miss the point Jesus is making here: on the Day of Judgment, there will be a final separation of all humanity. Some people will be called those 'who are blessed by my Father.' They will be welcomed into eternal life in heaven. Others are 'cursed' and will go into eternal punishment in hell. There are no other options. Unbelievers are judged for their rebellion against God, while God's people are rewarded for their faithful service because their sins have been paid for at the cross of Christ.

Let's ask some questions in order to understand this important subject:

WHAT IS HEAVEN?

Heaven is the place where God is particularly present in His love and holiness. Of course God is present in all places everywhere, but heaven is His special dwelling place (1 Kings 8:43, Isa. 66:1). This is why Jesus teaches us to pray to our Father 'in heaven' (Matt. 6:9). After His resurrection, Jesus went up into heaven (Heb. 9:24) and He is there even now, waiting for the day when He returns to the earth.

Heaven is a place where God is worshipped and delighted in (Rev. 4, Heb. 12:22–24). When a Christian dies, his or her spirit goes to be with Jesus in heaven (Phil. 1:21–23), where God has prepared a place for them to live in eternal happiness (Heb. 11:13–16). Heaven is a place of joy and blessing, where every temptation, tear, and trial is wiped away by God Himself (Rev. 21:4). No wonder Jesus calls it 'paradise' (Luke 23:43)! *Living with God in heaven is the greatest thing we have to look forward to.*

WHAT IS HELL?

Hell is a place of eternal punishment for those who refused to put their faith in Jesus and have therefore died in their sins (Eph. 5:3–6). In Revelation, John gives a terrifying vision of what happens to those who oppose the Lord:

'He also will drink the wine of God's wrath, poured full strength into the cup of his anger, and he will be tormented with fire and sulfur in the presence of the holy angels and in the presence of the Lamb. And the smoke of their torment goes up forever and ever, and they have no rest, day or night' (Rev. 14:10–11).

In short, hell is the worst fate we could ever imagine.

WHAT DOES HELL TEACH US?

Hell is a terrible reality, which is why some Christians have tried to water down the Bible's teaching to make it seem less awful.

+ Some have taught that hell is not a real place, but *a metaphor for the ways we ruin our lives through sin.*

+ Others have taught that hell is not eternal, but *a place where God puts sinners out of their misery by destroying them.*

+ Some church traditions have invented other options for humans after death—like 'purgatory,' where *our sins are cleansed and we're slowly prepared for heaven.*

- Still others say *hell is where God is absent and sinners are left to their own ways*. They're in hell because of their own free choice.

The main problem with these views is that they don't reflect what the Bible teaches. There may be elements of truth (for example, the consequences of our sin now *are* a taste of what hell will be like), but the Bible is clear that those who live in rebellion against God will experience unending suffering. In Mark's Gospel, Jesus called hell 'the unquenchable fire' and the place where 'the worm does not die and the fire is not quenched' (Mark 9:44 and 9:48). It's hard to understand what this means if not that the sufferings of hell go on forever.

This makes sense, too, for how could sin against an eternal God *not* be punished in an eternal way? If sin is treason committed by people with eternal souls against a perfectly holy God who exists in every place for all eternity, at what point in the future would we imagine that God's holy anger against sin will be finished?

We shouldn't act as if God's reputation and character need to be saved from the reality of hell. In fact, hell teaches us some important things—namely, that God is very holy and sin against Him is very terrible. *If the things that the Bible teaches about hell seem unfair or unjust, it's probably because we don't take God's glory and holiness seriously enough.* If we did, we wouldn't even think to suggest that God is somehow unjust to punish sin the way He does. In fact, it would be wrong for God *not* to punish sins the way He does.

STOP

Many people don't believe in a final judgment or in hell. What reasons might people have not to believe in these things?

WHAT DIFFERENCE DO HEAVEN AND HELL MAKE IN MY LIFE NOW?

Jesus spoke often about hell, not because He enjoyed scaring people but because He knew we ought to live in light of this terrible reality. We should be more concerned to avoid hell than to avoid suffering here on earth.

- *'If your right eye causes you to sin, tear it out and throw it away. For it is better that you lose one of your members than that your whole body be thrown into hell. And if your right hand causes you to sin, cut it off and throw it away. For it is better that you lose one of your members than that your whole body go into hell'* (Matt. 5:29–30).

- *'And do not fear those who kill the body but cannot kill the soul. Rather fear him who can destroy both soul and body in hell.'* (Matt. 10:28).

Thankfully, the opposite is also true. *If the reality of hell should keep us from sin, then the promise of heaven should encourage us toward holiness and obedience.*

- Pursuing purity might be tiresome and difficult, but there's an amazing reward waiting for us in heaven: *'Blessed are the pure in heart, for they shall see God'* (Matt. 5:8).

- The author of Hebrews tells us that Moses said 'no' to the sinful pleasures of Egypt in order to obtain a reward in heaven: *'By faith Moses, when he was grown up, refused to be called the son of Pharaoh's daughter, choosing rather to be mistreated with the people of God than to enjoy the fleeting pleasures of sin. He considered the reproach of Christ greater wealth than the treasures of Egypt, for he was looking to the reward'* (Heb. 11:24–26).

ILLUSTRATION

Knowing the consequences of certain behaviours helps us make good decisions. People used to smoke cigarettes like crazy. Now that we know they cause lung cancer, far fewer people are willing to smoke. The cost is simply too high. People choose not to break laws simply because they don't want to go to jail. Knowing that hell awaits for those who live in rebellion against God should motivate us to say 'no' to sin and to be reconciled to God through faith in Jesus.

Similarly, most people are willing to experience some kind of short-term difficulty in order to gain something better in the future. People go to work, lift weights, eat healthy foods, stay in school, and save money not because those are the most enjoyable things in the moment, but because they bring long-term rewards that are worth the short-term sacrifices. Heaven is like that; it's our long-term reward. We bypass sinful pleasures because we know it's far better to have heaven than to have the fleeting enjoyment of sin.

The Bible is very realistic; it never says that sin brings no pleasure. After all, there are reasons people do sinful things!

Getting high feels good in the moment.

Stealing money enables you to buy things you'll enjoy.

Sexual sin brings physical pleasure.

We don't need to deny this truth in order to avoid sin.

But here's the problem with sin: *its pleasures are too small and too temporary.* Whatever moment of happiness we get can never make hell worth it; they can't compare to the eternal joys of being in God's presence forever.

SAMUEL

At first, the idea of eternal punishment made Samuel uncomfortable. But as he thought about it, the world he knew was filled with injustice. The strong always took advantage of the weak, men preyed on women, adults used children, and the wicked took advantage of the good. In this light, it became easier to see the goodness in God's just judgment.

MEMORY VERSE

'These all died in faith, not having received the things promised, but having seen them and greeted them from afar, and having acknowledged that they were strangers and exiles on the earth. For people who speak thus make it clear that they are seeking a homeland. If they had been thinking of that land from which they had gone out, they would have had opportunity to return. But as it is, they desire a better country, that is, a heavenly one. Therefore God is not ashamed to be called their God, for he has prepared for them a city' (Heb. 11:13–16).

SUMMARY

Because we were made by God in His image, every human being is ultimately accountable to Him. God has promised to punish sins for all eternity in hell, but has also promised to give eternal life in paradise to everyone who turns to Him through faith in Christ. Those truths should motivate us to say 'no' to sin and to look forward to being with God in heaven.

WHAT'S THE POINT?

When Jesus returns, everything is going to change forever.

9. JESUS' RETURN

We've covered a lot of ground so far: God's character, the creation of the world, mankind's fall into sin, redemption through Jesus Christ, and the reality of heaven and hell. We're left with just one more topic to cover: Christ's return.

 SAMUEL

> If Samuel is being totally honest, sometimes he finds it a bit difficult to believe all of the things the Bible teaches. After all, he doesn't talk to Jesus or walk around with Him. It requires a lot of faith to put your hope in someone you can't see, and for 2,000 years Christians have lived 'by faith' and not 'by sight.'

But one day all of that will change.

JESUS IS COMING BACK

After Jesus rose from the dead, He spent forty days with His disciples before going up into heaven to take His place of honour. Once He'd ascended into heaven, the disciples received a promise that one day He would return:

'And while they were gazing into heaven as he went, behold, two men stood by them in white robes, and said, "Men of Galilee, why do you stand looking into heaven? This Jesus, who was taken up from

you into heaven, will come in the same way as you saw him go into heaven'" (Acts 1:10–11).

This shouldn't have surprised them, for Jesus had often taught about this. We find one instance in Matthew 24, where Jesus speaks of Himself as 'The Son of Man' and says:

'Then will appear in heaven the sign of the Son of Man, and then all the tribes of the earth will mourn, and they will see the Son of Man coming on the clouds of heaven with power and great glory. And he will send out his angels with a loud trumpet call, and they will gather his elect from the four winds, from one end of heaven to the other' (Matt. 24:30–31).

In fact, all throughout the letters of the New Testament, the authors assume it's important for us to know that Jesus will return. For example, Paul wrote to the Thessalonians: *'For the Lord himself will descend with a cry of command, with the voice of an archangel, and with the sound of the trumpet of God. And the dead will rise in Christ first'* (1 Thess. 4:16).

Let's take a look at a few important things we should know about Jesus' return.

JESUS' SECOND COMING WILL BE DIFFERENT FROM HIS FIRST COMING

When Jesus came to earth the first time, He was a picture of humility and lowliness. He was born into humble circumstances and lived in poverty. There was nothing unusual about His appearance that would have made you think He was anything special. When He came the first time, most people had absolutely no idea that anything significant had happened.

But His second coming won't be like that at all. As we've already seen it will be with 'great power and glory' (Matt. 24:30). When

Jesus returns, it will be a spectacle that the whole world will see. In Matthew's Gospel, Jesus told His disciples not to believe anyone who claims to have seen Jesus return to earth because everyone will know without a doubt when He actually does come back. It's not something that can be missed:

'So, if they say to you, "Look, he is in the wilderness," do not go out. If they say, "Look, he is in the inner rooms," do not believe it. For as the lightning comes from the east and shines as far as the west, so will be the coming of the Son of Man' (Matt. 24:26–27).

Jesus came to earth the first time in order to suffer and save sinful people, but at His second coming He will bring judgment to the world. In Matthew 16:27, we read: 'For the Son of Man is going to come with his angels in the glory of his Father, and then he will repay each person according to what he has done.' And in Revelation 22:12, Jesus says, 'Behold, I am coming soon, bringing my recompense with me, to repay each one for what he has done.'

When we appear before Jesus in judgment, a great separation will take place. All people will be raised from the dead, but there will be two very different fates awaiting them. Followers of Christ won't be condemned for their sins (Rom. 8:1) because Jesus has already taken their judgment and condemnation at the cross. Instead, they'll receive gracious rewards from God for their acts of love and obedience (2 Cor. 5:10). Unbelievers, however, will be held accountable for their rebellion against God and will receive the just punishment for their actions (see the previous chapter's discussion of hell).

THERE WILL BE SIGNS...

The main questions people today ask when they think about Jesus' return are 'when is it going to happen?' and 'how can I know when it's coming?' Interestingly, people asked these same questions while Jesus was still on earth. In fact, Jesus told His disciples about some of the signs that would lead up to His return. Some of those things were fulfilled while the disciples were still alive (like the destruction of the temple and the city of Jerusalem by the Romans back in 70 AD, see Mark 13:1–18), but others wouldn't occur until immediately before Jesus' return (like the sun being darkened and the stars falling from heaven, see Mark 13:24–26).

... BUT WE DON'T KNOW WHEN

It seems that every so often a crazy Bible teacher decides he has cracked the Bible's code and he found out when Jesus is coming back. But they're always wrong because Jesus Himself said only God the Father knows the day and hour of His return. Even Jesus Himself says He doesn't know when He's going to come back!

It's sad how many Christians waste so much time and energy by trying to figure out whether certain current events—a war, an earthquake, the rise of a threatening political leader—will precede Jesus' imminent return. The New Testament never encourages this kind of speculation. Instead, it offers a sobering truth about the future that should impact the way we live in the present.

In Mark 13, Jesus warned His followers about how they ought to live in light of His return. Speaking of the timing, Jesus said:

'But concerning that day or that hour, no one knows, not even the angels in heaven, nor the Son, but only the Father. Be on guard, keep awake. For you do not know when the time will come. It is like a man going on a journey, when he leaves home and puts his servants in charge, each with his work, and commands the doorkeeper to stay awake. Therefore stay awake—for you do not know when the master of the house will come, in the evening, or at midnight, or when the rooster crows, or in the morning—lest he come suddenly and find you asleep. And what I say to you I say to all: Stay awake' (Mark 13:32–37).

It's not too hard to understand what Jesus is saying here. No one knows when He will return; therefore, we ought to live each day with expectation (because we know that He *will* return) and uncertainty (because we do not know *when* He will return).

 ILLUSTRATION

Imagine your friend went away for a while and allowed you to stay at his house. You made yourself comfortable and had a nice time. But now, your friend is coming home and the house isn't ready. You have food containers all over the place, your dirty clothes are everywhere, and the whole house smells like sweat. You'd rush around like crazy trying to clean up, or else your friend would be offended by your lack of care.

Well, Jesus has left us on earth with expectations for how we'll live in His absence. Since He could return at any moment, there won't be time to prepare for His arrival. That's a good reason to make sure you're living every day in such a way as to be ready for His return.

STOP

What do you think it means to be ready for Jesus' return? What things do you think He wants us to be doing while He is 'away'? What things should we *not* be doing?

 'For you yourselves are fully aware that the day of the Lord will come like a thief in the night. While people are saying, "There is peace and security," then sudden destruction will come upon them as labor pains come upon a pregnant woman, and they will not escape. But you are not in darkness, brothers, for that day to surprise you like a thief. For you are all children of light, children of the day. We are not of the night or of the darkness. So then let us not sleep, as others do, but let us keep awake and be sober. For those who sleep, sleep at night, and those who get drunk, are drunk at night. But since we belong to the day, let us be

sober, having put on the breastplate of faith and love, and for a helmet the hope of salvation' (1 Thess. 5:2–8).

WHAT HAPPENS AFTER JUDGMENT?

Jesus' return will bring the history of the world to a sudden and dramatic end. Every deed by every person in every age will be brought to light and judged.

But this end will actually just be the beginning of a magnificent new world. Here's what the Bible says happens next:

1. **The old world will be put away.** In 2 Peter 3, we read: *'But the day of the Lord will come like a thief, and then the heavens will pass away with a roar, and the heavenly bodies will be burned up and dissolved, and the earth and the works that are done on it will be exposed'* (2 Pet. 3:10).

2. **God will bring a new heaven and a new earth.** All the way back in the Old Testament, in Isaiah 65, God promised that He would make new heavens and a new earth. At the end of the Bible, in Revelation 21, the Apostle John saw the fulfilment of that promise:

'Then I saw a new heaven and a new earth, for the first heaven and the first earth had passed away, and the sea was no more. And I saw the holy city, new Jerusalem, coming down out of heaven from God, prepared as a bride adorned for her husband. And I heard a loud voice from the throne saying, "Behold, the dwelling place of God is with man. He will dwell with them, and they will be his people, and God himself will be with them as their God. He will wipe away every tear from their eyes, and death shall be no more, neither shall there be mourning, nor crying, nor pain anymore, for the former things have passed away"' (Rev. 21: 1-4).

As people who live in a world marred by sin and suffering, it's hard to even imagine what this kind of place would be like. But it offers a marvellous hope that one day we'll no longer experience pain, regret, and sin. One day, all those sad and sinful things will merely be 'former things.'

3. **We will live with God forever.** When believers die, their souls go immediately to be in God's presence in heaven (Phil. 1:23, Luke 23:43). When Jesus returns, we'll receive 'glorified' bodies that are not subject to sin, death, and disease. We'll live in these perfect, sinless bodies with God for all eternity, just as we were created to do. God will dwell in our midst, and we will be in His presence.

SAMUEL

Samuel's life is difficult. But when he reflects on the fact that his problems will not last forever, he is encouraged to persevere. One day, all his troubles and struggles will be gone, and he will be with God forever. Until that day, he can keep walking with Jesus and looking forward to His return.

MEMORY VERSE

'He who testifies to these things says, "Surely I am coming soon." Amen. Come, Lord Jesus!' (Rev. 22:20).

SUMMARY

The Bible began with mankind in paradise amidst the presence of God. There was no sin and no death. When Adam and Even sinned, this perfection was lost. But at the end of the Bible, we see that God had planned all along to restore us to that kind of life in that kind of world. As if that were not enough, there's more great news! Not only will we spend eternity with God in paradise, but (unlike the Garden of Eden) we can never lose out on this paradise, for there will be no sin, no temptation, and no tears.

9Marks

This series of short workbooks, from the 9Marks series, are designed to help you think through some of life's big questions.

1. GOD: Is He Out There?

2. WAR: Why Did Life Just Get Harder?

3. VOICES: Who Am I Listening To?

4. BIBLE: Can We Trust It?

5. BELIEVE: What Should I Know?

6. CHARACTER: How Do I Change?

7. TRAINING: How Do I Live and Grow?

8. CHURCH: Do I Have To Go?

9. RELATIONSHIPS: How Do I Make Things Right?

10. SERVICE: How Do I Give Back?

9Marks

Building Healthy Churches

9Marks exists to equip church leaders with a biblical vision and practical resources for displaying God's glory to the nations through healthy churches.

To that end, we want to see churches characterized by these nine marks of health:

1   Expositional Preaching
2   Biblical Theology
3   A Biblical Understanding of the Gospel
4   A Biblical Understanding of Conversion
5   A Biblical Understanding of Evangelism
6   Biblical Church Membership
7   Biblical Church Discipline
8   Biblical Discipleship
9   Biblical Church Leadership

Find more titles at

www.9Marks.org

2✝schemes
Gospel Churches for Scotland's Poorest

20schemes exists to bring gospel hope to Scotland's poorest communities through the revitalisation and planting of healthy, gospel-preaching churches, ultimately led by a future generation of indigenous church leaders.

> *'If we are really going to see a turnaround in the lives of residents in our poorest communities, then we have to embrace a radical and long-term strategy which will bring gospel-hope to untold thousands.'*

MEZ MCCONNELL, Ministry Director

We believe that building healthy churches in Scotland's poorest communities will bring true, sustainable, and long-term renewal to countless lives.

THE NEED IS URGENT

Learn more about our work and how to partner with us at:

20SCHEMES.COM
TWITTER.COM/20SCHEMES
FACEBOOK.COM/20SCHEMES
INSTAGRAM.COM/20SCHEMES